The Parable of
the Seeds

Matthew 13:1–23; Mark 4:1–20; and Luke 8:4–15
for children

Written by Joanne Bader

Illustrated by Dana Regan

D1472539

CONCORDIA PUBLISHING HOUSE · SAINT LOUIS

One day, when Jesus stepped outside
To sit beside the sea,
A crowd of people gathered round,
Excited as could be!

They pushed and shoved to get in close
To hear what He would say,
So He climbed in a nearby boat,
Sat down, and spoke that way.

The people stood along the beach
List'ning to what He said.
His story, called a "parable,"
Told how His Word is spread.

He talked about a farmer who
Took seed outside to sow,
But some seed fell along the path.
Alas, it did not grow.

First, people walked all over it;
Then, hungry birds flew by.
They swooped down and devoured it
And soared into the sky.

Some seeds fell down on rocky ground
Where there was not much dirt.
Green shoots poked up immediately,
But soon, these plants were hurt.

The sun came out and scorched the leaves—
The soil there was so thin.
And since there was no moisture there,
The roots could not dig in!

Now, some seeds fell among the thorns,
Where they just could not sprout.
Because the weeds grew thick and tall,
The new plants were choked out.

But some seeds fell on good, rich soil,
And they took root and grew.
Their stalks produced so much more grain
Than folks thought they could do.

When the parable was finished,
Jesus made it quite clear
That all who were there listening
Should use their ears to hear.

After the crowd left to go home,
His followers cried out,
"Why do You speak in parables?
What are they all about?"

"The sower speaks the Word of God,"
Jesus quickly replied.
"Just like the seeds fell everywhere,
God's Word goes far and wide.

"The seeds that dropped along the path
Are like words people hear.
But if they do not understand,
The words soon disappear.

"The seeds that bounced on rocky ground
Or tumbled to the weeds
Are words that folks hear and forget,
Choked out by their own needs.

"The seeds that landed in rich soil
Are like the words God sows
In hearts of people everywhere
So that His Word then grows."

Now, let your heart be like good soil,
And open your ears too,
So when you hear the Word of God,
It roots and grows in you!

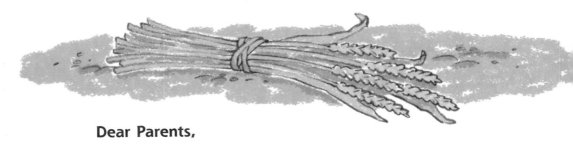

Dear Parents,

Jesus was a wonderful storyteller. He often used special short stories, or parables, about everyday people and events to illustrate a spiritual truth. It was His way of telling the listeners about the Gospel and the spread of His kingdom here on earth, about His love and forgiveness, about how He answers prayers, or about how God wants Christians to live.

The focus of this parable is the spread of God's kingdom. The seeds of God's Word invite people everywhere to open their ears to hear, nurturing faith in Him. However, the temptation of the devil, the world, and our own sinful flesh lead many people to resist the words they hear. Therefore, the Good News of the Gospel does not take root in their hearts or grow.

As Christians, we continue to share the Word with others and to pray that their ears will be open to hear God's Word so faith will grow in their hearts. Pray with your children also, that they "open their ears and hear."

To Him be the glory!

The Author

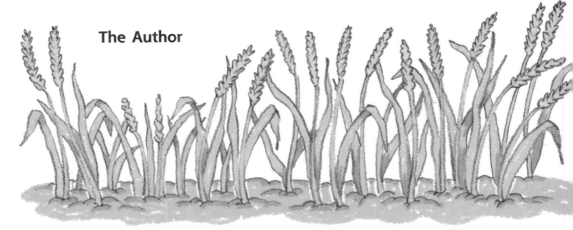